TV and MOVIE TIE-INS

MORK & MINDY

by Paul D. Schneck

Creative Education, Inc.
Mankato, Minnesota

Published by Creative Education, 123 South Broad Street, Mankato, Minnesota 56001.

Photography:
Wide World Photos . . . . pages 4, 7, 13, 19, 31
Globe Photos
   Bruce Birmelin . . . . pages 8, 32
   Cutler . . . . page 24
   Ralph Dominguez . . . . pages 16, 23, 26, 29, 30
   Donald Sanders . . . . page 20 and cover
   Steve Schatzberg . . . . page 15

Library of Congress Number: 80-16985   ISBN: 0-87191-754-8

Library of Congress Cataloging in Publication Data
Schneck, Paul D.   Mork & Mindy

SUMMARY: Discusses the popular TV show, "Mork and Mindy," and its two stars. 1. Mork & Mindy (Television program)—Juvenile literature. 2. Williams, Robin, 1952- —Juvenile literature. 3. Dawber, Pam, 1951- —Juvenile literature. 4. Television personalities—United States—Biography—Juvenile literature. [1. Mork & Mindy (Television program) 2. Williams, Robin, 1952- 3. Dawber, Pam, 1951- 4. Actors and actresses] I. Mork & Mindy (Television program) II. Title. III. Series.
PN1992.77.M66S3   791.45'72   80.16985 ⫯
ISBN 0-87191-754-8

A Weird Beginning

A six-foot egg floats through outer-space. Landing one night near Boulder, Colorado, the egg suddenly begins to hatch. First a small crack appears. Then the crack grows bigger. A fist pushes through. Finally, the egg falls open and out steps a man dressed in funny-looking clothes.

But this isn't just any egg. It's a space-craft shaped like an egg. And as millions of television fans can tell you, this egg comes from outer-space, from the planet Ork. The spaceman is named Mork. Mork from Ork.

From this weird beginning comes one of the most popular characters in television history and today's number-one show, *Mork and Mindy*.

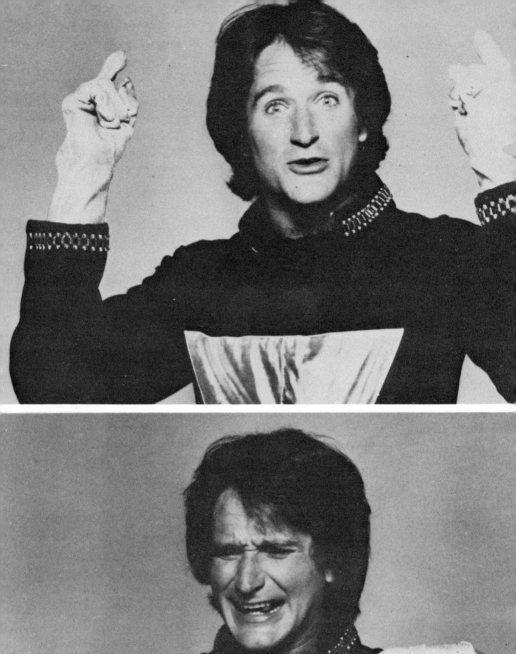

Except for Mork,
Orkans show no emotion.

For the one or two people in the world who don't know, Mork has been sent to Earth to see if Orkans can live here. The Orkans, you see, will someday have to leave their own planet.

Mork was also sent to Earth as a punishment. Except for Mork, Orkans show no emotion. They don't get happy or sad, cry, laugh or even tell jokes. Mork does these things all the time— especially jokes.

He makes up funny names for his leader, an Orkan named Orson. Mork has been known to call Orson "Fatso," "Rocketship Thighs" and "Star Tush."

Mork is supposed to learn all he can about Earth. Fortunately for him, he meets a very nice and very pretty Earth woman named Mindy McConnel.

Mindy lives in Boulder, working and going to school. At first she doesn't believe Mork is really a space traveler.

Mork says *Na-No, Na-No* to Mindy, which is Orkan for "hello." He takes pictures of her— using his glowing hand for a flashcube! She gives him a drink and Mork sticks his finger in the glass. The drink disappears as Mork uses his fingers as a straw!

Nevertheless, she still doesn't believe he's from outer-space. Finally, Mork's luggage arrives. When there's a knock at her apartment door, Mindy opens it to find another egg floating in the air. Mork opens the egg's top and takes out his suitcase. This does it. Mindy finally believes Mork is really from Ork, in outer-space.

And we believe him, too. Just a week after its premiere, *Mork and Mindy* was already the number one show on television, replacing previous favorites, *Happy Days* and *Laverne and Shirley*.

Just a week after its premiere, *Mork and Mindy* was already the number one show.

Many things make *Mork and Mindy* the
fantastically popular show that it is. The two most
important reasons are the show's stars, Robin
Williams and Pam Dawber. And yet as famous as
they are now, Robin and Pam were almost
unknown before *Mork and Mindy.*

Robin had been trying to make it as a comedian in Los Angeles and San Francisco. He performed at night clubs and appeared regularly in the new *Laugh-In* shows. Sometimes he worked for free. He performed often at The Comedy Store in Los Angeles, a club where famous and unknown comedians try out new material. One of his fellow-performers from those days was John Ritter, now the well-known star of *Three's Company*.

It's Robin's humor that makes *Mork and Mindy* come alive. It's infectious, new and fresh. But, most of all, it's just good clean fun. Robin doesn't make us laugh by putting people down or making fun of them. He doesn't make us laugh by swearing. Instead, he uses funny sounds, weird body movements and strange voices that simply drive us crazy.

As Mork, Robin pokes fun at some of the sad things in our world. He does this by looking at sad things through the innocent eyes of a young child. Being from outer-space, Mork hasn't had time to learn about loneliness, greed, hate or war.

At the end of each show, Mork talks with Orson about what he's learned on Earth. He often tries to describe some of the sad and difficult things he's experienced. For instance, in one show Mork explains loneliness to Orson. Everyone is lonely, Mork tells Orson. If they just told each other about it, Mork suggests, they wouldn't be so lonely. In this fresh and simple way, Mork helps us learn about ourselves.

Robin auditioned for the Mork role along with nineteen or twenty other actors. He just got up in front of the camera and did his thing—weird sounds and voices—and the job was his! In fact, he had already included a space-man in his nightclub act, so the Mork role came to him naturally.

In a fresh and simple way,
Mork helps us learn about ourselves.

Pam, meanwhile, won the Mindy role in a different manner. She was living in New York and then decided to go to audition for the lead role in the *Tabitha* television series. Luckily, she didn't get the part, because the show was a failure.

After casting Robin as Mork, the producers of *Mork and Mindy* began looking hard for someone to play Mindy. One day they came across a tape of Pam's *Tabitha* audition. Something about Pam appealed to them.

They spliced the *Tabitha* tape with a tape of Robin as Mork, and it was like magic. Robin and Pam were made for each other!

Yet Pam knew nothing of these events. You can imagine her surprise when, leafing through the newspaper one afternoon, she read that she had been cast as Mindy!

Robin and Pam have now become famous. Strangely enough, they were practically neighbors. They grew up within fifteen miles of each other, near Detroit, Michigan.

Robin Into Mork

Robin was born on July 21, 1952. Since his parents each had an older child from previous marriages, Robin grew up almost as an only child.

The family lived in a thirty-room mansion in Bloomfield Hill, a suburb of Detroit. Robin's dad worked for Ford Motor Company. Spending a lot of time alone in the big house, Robin became his own best friend. He'd invent imaginary characters and give them funny voices and strange faces— all to amuse himself. Probably the closest things to friends were his two thousand toy soldiers. Sometimes, he staged huge battles between his soldiers, using his own voice to create sound effects.

Robin was very shy. He was also fat, and eventually his schoolmates began to make fun of him. Sometimes they called him nicknames like "Dwarf" and "Leprechaun."

Finally, Robin had had about as much as he could stand. He took up wrestling and lost thirty pounds. He also began making people laugh—he discovered it was a good way to make friends. By the time Robin's father retired and the family moved to Northern California, Robin had changed so much he was voted "Funniest" at Redwood High School.

Stand-up comics were Robin's heroes. Jonathan Winters, with his strange sounds and faces, was a favorite. Robin especially loved the funny characters Winters invents and acts out. Most of us know Jonathan Winters for his hilarious plastic trash bag commercials.

Peter Sellers was another favorite of Robin's. Sellers also uses faces and sounds to make us laugh. He's best known for his role as the zany Inspector Cleuseau, in the Pink Panther movies.

Robin's other big hero was Woody Allen. In fact, Robin says someday he'd like to do the kind of movie that Allen is famous for.

Stand-up comics were Robin's heroes.

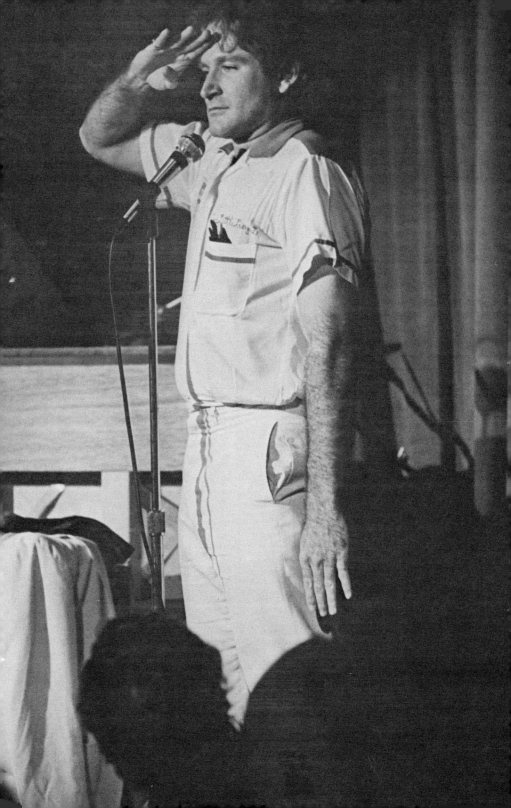

In college, Robin started studying political science. But he took one course in drama and that was it—he was hooked on performing. After that, he went to the Julliard School in New York and studied with John Houseman, Academy Award winner for his role in *The Paper Chase.*

Three years later, Robin was back in San Francisco, working in small nightclubs or performing in the city's amazing street theatre. Tourists there can see street performances of magicians, mimes, comics, puppeteers and just about anything else you can imagine.

But street comedy didn't pay much, so Robin also tended bar at a nightclub. Working at the same club was a pretty waitress named Valerie Velardi. Valerie, who is a modern dancer, was instantly fascinated by the funny bartender and his many changing faces. Not long afterward, the funny bartender and the modern dancer fell in love and were married.

Valerie knew that Robin was very talented and soon she convinced him to move to Los Angeles and try to make it in Hollywood. Without Valerie's confidence in Robin, Mork as we know him might never have been.

Pam Into Mindy

Pam Dawber also grew up near Detroit, in Farmington, Michigan. She was born on October 18, 1951. Her mother, Thelma, operates a stock photo company and her father, Gene, is a commercial artist.

Pam's parents taught her early to appreciate the arts. She took flute lessons, as well as guitar and ballet. Even now, her two favorite pastimes are singing and painting.

Like Robin, Pam also moved to northern California. She went to Oakland Community College and began to take modeling jobs in nearby San Francisco.

Pam's modeling was so successful that she decided to leave school and move to New York City. One day when a girlfriend had an appointment with a modeling agency, Pam went along for fun. She was hired instantly and soon was getting work with all the top fashion magazines. She even began doing television commercials.

The commercials led to more acting work. Soon she had won a few theatre and small movie roles. Pam's big break came when she landed a

small role in Robert Altman's movie, *A Wedding*. When the call came to go to Hollywood for the *Tabitha* audition, Pam was ready.

Not all of Pam's life has been happy, however. Her younger sister Leslie died during open-heart surgery. Six other family members died within a three-year span. Because of these tragedies, perhaps, Pam is a very private person and values her time alone. Although she has apartments in both New York City and Los Angeles, she still considers her real home to be a frontier-like cabin in upstate New York's Catskill Mountains.

Robin and Pam have become enormously popular stars after leading remarkably parallel lives. *Mork and Mindy* is one of the hottest shows to ever hit television. We know how Robin and Pam became Mork and Mindy, but where did the idea for Mork and Mindy come from?

Fonzie's Dream

Ideas for hit television shows come from different sources, but not many come from nine-year-olds. Well, that's exactly how *Mork and Mindy* began.

It all started with the space craze that's been sweeping the country for the past few years. The movie, *Star Wars*, was probably the first phase in this space excitement. It became one of the most popular movies in history. Next came *Close Encounters of A Third Kind*, another popular space-oriented movie.

Next thing *Happy Days* fans knew,
Fonzie was dreaming of a
funny spaceman who did weird things...

Enter Scotti Marshall, the nine-year-old son of Garry Marshall. Garry is the successful producer of *Happy Days* and *Laverne and Shirley*. Scotti is one of those kids who saw *Star Wars* many times—a real space freak.

Scotti thought a man from outer space should make an appearance on *Happy Days*. So he made the suggestion to his dad. Next thing *Happy Days* fans knew, Fonzie was dreaming of a funny spaceman who did weird things. It was · Robin's first appearance as Mork.

The response from the fans was instantaneous. There were so many letters and phone calls that Garry Marshall had no trouble deciding to do a series based on the funny spaceman. They didn't even bother to make a pilot first—that's how popular Mork had already become.

Living With Stardom

Now in their second year as stars of TV's Number One show, Robin Williams and Pam Dawber are both trying hard to stay themselves. Neither one wants to turn into a typical movie star.

Robin is best known for his humor, of course, but his wardrobe has also become popular with fans. He wears British Air Force trousers, three-inch wide multi-colored suspenders, old shirts and shabby tennis shoes. His suspenders are covered with pins and emblems. A sheriff's badge on one side, on the other a porpoise and a one-legged toad.

Now, if you're a Mork fan (and who isn't?), you're probably thinking these clothes sound just like his Mork wardrobe. Well, you're right. That's because Robin wears the same thing to play Mork that he wears when he's just being Robin Williams!

Robin and Valerie live in a simple three-room apartment. They also own a small beach-house. They don't have any children, but they do have roommates.

One roommate is a lizard named Truman Capote. There's also an iguana named Mister E. (Sounds like "Mystery." Get it?) And finally, there's Cora, a talking parrot. In keeping with Robin's whacky sense of humor, Cora's only line is "Birds can't talk!"

Robin's future looks bright, even brilliant. He plans to do television specials, guest spots and at least three more years as Mork. He's also beginning work on his first starring movie role as the lead in *Popeye.* Robin's funny faces and strange sounds should be perfect for recreating the famous, lovable, and comical spinach-eating sailor.

Robin's future looks bright, even brilliant...

He's also beginning work on
his first starring movie role
as lead in *Popeye.*

Pam Dawber also has plans for the future, but
they center around her desire to be herself. She
spends as much time as she can at her cabin in
the Catskills. There she can snow-ski in the
winter and water-ski, canoe, ride horseback and
swim in the warmer months. Pam also enjoys
cooking and has an avid interest in health foods
and nutrition.

Pam and Robin work well together. Their good chemistry is probably the reason *Mork and Mindy* is so popular. Robin, of course, is the funny man. During the filming of the show, his constant adlibs and spontaneous antics keep the crew and rest of the cast always laughing.

Mindy is the straight-woman who balances Mork's zany humor. Her role brings consistency and warmth to the show. And, of course, there's always a hint of romance between Mork and Mindy.

After watching a few episodes, fans soon catch on to Orkan language. *Na-no, Na-no* means hello, of course. But it also means goodbye. *Shazbot!* is a kind of swear word, like "darn!" *Nimnul* is Orkan for "dummy." *Grebbels* and *brandels* are Orkan money. And *krell* is a period of time on Ork, equal to 5000 earth-years.

So, *Na-no, Na-no,* Mork fans, see you in a couple *krells.* And watch *Mork and Mindy* unless you're a *nimnul!*

Shazbot!!